Praise for
101 Cups of Water

"Refreshingly honest and disarmingly vulnerable."

—CECIL MURPHEY, best-selling coauthor of *90 Minutes in Heaven* and *Heaven Is Real*

"C. D. Baker shows us all the surprising times and places we can drink from God's cup."

—LUCI SHAW, poet and author of *Breath for the Bones, The Crime of Living Cautiously,* and *Accompanied by Angels*; writer in residence at Regent College

"Every soul can find rest and peace in these perfect little sips."

—RAY BLACKSTON, author of *Flabbergasted*

"David Baker invites readers into a perilous journey to the headwaters. You will find your preconceived notions of Christianity challenged, your veneer of pretense sanded down, and the bare wood of your thirsty soul exposed. These brief devotional readings strip away the facade and take us honestly to our longing for Living Water—and the quenching of your thirsty soul. Come—take and drink these surprisingly deep little cups of fresh, clear water for your soul."

—JANE RUBIETTA, author of *Come Closer: A Call to Life, Love, and Breakfast on the Beach*

These cups belong to

_____

presented on this day of

_____

by

_____

101 cups of water

relief and refreshment for the tired, thirsty soul

c.d. baker

WATERBROOK
PRESS

101 CUPS OF WATER
PUBLISHED BY WATERBROOK PRESS
12265 Oracle Boulevard, Suite 200
Colorado Springs, Colorado 80921
A division of Random House Inc.

ISBN 978-1-4000-7399-3

Published in association with the literary agency of Alive Communications Inc., 7680
Goddard Street, Suite 200, Colorado Springs, CO 80920, www.alivecommunications.com

Library of Congress Cataloging-in-Publication Data
Baker, C. D. (Charles David), 1951–
   101 cups of water : relief and refreshment for the tired, thirsty soul / C.D. Baker.
— 1st ed.
     p. cm.
  Includes index.
  ISBN 978-1-4000-7399-3
   1. Consolation. 2. Encouragement—Religious aspects—Christianity. 3. Christian
life—Meditations. I. Title. II. Title: One hundred one cups of water. III. Title: One
hundred and one cups of water.
  BV4909.B35 2008
  242—dc22

                            2007036230

Printed in the United States of America
2008—First Edition

10 9 8 7 6 5 4 3 2

contents

Tired? Thirsty? Welcome 1

A Cup of Grace 5
A Cup of Significance 7
A Cup of Abundance 9
A Cup of Dependence 11
A Cup of Un-Knowing 13
A Cup of Freedom 15
A Cup of Comfort 17
A Cup of Easy 19
A Cup of Self-Control 21
A Cup of Identity 23
A Cup of Appreciation 25
A Cup of Honesty 27
A Cup of Security 29
A Cup of Clinging 31
A Cup of Humility 33
A Cup of Quiet 35
A Cup of Righteousness 37
A Cup of Faith 39
A Cup of Adoption 41
A Cup of Focus 43

A Cup of Love 45

A Cup of Forgiveness 47

A Cup of Mystery 49

A Cup of Un-Control 51

A Cup of Christ-Esteem 53

A Cup of Weakness 55

A Cup of Trust 57

A Cup of Others 59

A Cup of Possibility 61

A Cup of Hope 63

A Cup of Glad 65

A Cup of Tomorrow 67

A Cup of Amazing 69

A Cup of Excitement 71

A Cup of Safety 73

A Cup of Opportunity 75

A Cup of Strength 77

A Cup of All's Well 79

A Cup of Good Fruit 81

A Cup of Plenty 83

A Cup of Surprise 85

A Cup of Air 87

A Cup of Waiting 89

A Cup of Liberation 91

A Cup of Clarity 93

A Cup of Secrets 95

A Cup of Beloving 97

A Cup of Release 99

A Cup of the Spirit 101

A Cup of Who Cares? 103

A Cup of Courage 105

A Cup of Reality 107

A Cup of Approval 109

A Cup of Order 111

A Cup of Truth 113

A Cup of Providence 115

A Cup of Letting Go 117

A Cup of Defiance 119

A Cup of Sanity 121

A Cup of Devotion 123

A Cup of Direction 125

A Cup of Noise 127

A Cup of Powerlessness 129

A Cup of Companionship 131

A Cup of Holiness 133

A Cup of Happy 135

A Cup of Contentment 137

A Cup of Life 139

A Cup of Redemption 141

A Cup of Rest 143

A Cup of God's Presence 145

A Cup of Openness 147

A Cup of Feel-Good 149

A Cup of Stillness 151

A Cup of Salvation 153

A Cup of Friendship 155

A Cup of Self-Awareness 157

A Cup of Confidence 159

A Cup of Confession 161

A Cup of Relief 163

A Cup of Desperate Wonder 165

A Cup of Responsibility 167

A Cup of Want-To 169

A Cup of Warning 171

A Cup of Already 173

A Cup of Prayer 175

A Cup of Care 177

A Cup of Health 179

A Cup of Power 181

A Cup of Certainty 183

A Cup of Abandon 185

A Cup of Meekness 187

A Cup of Goodness 189

A Cup of Goal Management 191

A Cup of Vulnerability 193

A Cup of Boldness 195

A Cup of Motivation 197

A Cup of Relaxation 199

A Cup of Discernment 201
A Cup of the Way 203
A Cup of Thanksgiving 205

Acknowledgments 206
Index of First Lines 207

For my grandmother, Ruth

Tired? Thirsty?
Welcome

Dear Christian,

Has trying harder to succeed in the Christian life made you:

- too intense to be loving?
- too shamed to feel joy?
- too frustrated to be at peace?
- too self-absorbed to be patient?
- too disappointed to be kind?
- too angry to be good?
- too fearful to be faithful?
- too defensive to be meek?
- too worn out to be self-controlled?

If so, you're probably a prisoner of good intentions. Like so many other folks, you've been left thirsting for another way.

God intended his children to live an abundant life of relationship with him, one without self-effort and the inevitable fatigue it brings. Adopted out of the courtroom, we're set free to enjoy the warmth and wonders of our Father's house. Yet most of us have not danced in his gardens or laughed with Jesus for a very long time—in large part because we haven't been shown how. We've not rested in the shade of his kindness nor dined on his bounty because many in the church have unwittingly encouraged us to try harder at the Christian life. So we find ourselves discouraged, exhausted, and bound to expectations that weigh us down with guilt and shame.

The 101 reflections in this book are designed to bring comfort to weary Christians. They're based on the experiences and insights of struggling believers who have drawn deeply from the well of grace. Therefore, although my name appears as the author, the primary sources of inspiration have been others for whom I speak. A particular contributor has been my good friend and mentor, David McCarty, the founder of a discipling ministry known as Gospel-Friendships Inc.

I hope you'll find each reflection to be an honest look at our Christian walk, one that points you toward the astonishing gospel of Jesus, where the parched souls of God's children are refreshed unconditionally by the cool streams of the Father's love.

Sip slowly.

Enjoy.

And let's help each other remember the promise: "Whoever drinks of the water that I [Jesus] will give him shall never thirst; but the water that I will give him will become in him a well of water springing up to eternal life" (John 4:14).

Grace and peace be with you always,

C. D. Baker

101 cups of water

a cup of grace

I can't live the Christian life.

Don't tell anyone, but I've tried and I've tried and I can't. I haven't loved God with all my heart, soul, and mind, and I certainly haven't loved my neighbors as myself. It's that simple.

The Big Lie that's weighed so heavily on me is that I can make my Christian life "work." It's a lie that has stood in the way of my enjoying true communion with God, a lie that's kept me from more fully appreciating the beauty of the creation around me and the community of others.

So, yes, I admit that I can't make my Christian life work.

Praise be to God, who has freed me from the trying.

He's shown me that only Christ can live the Christian life, and he lives that life through me more fully as I get that trying-harder Self out of his way (Galatians 3).

So what do I do? I ask the Holy Spirit to show me my weakness, my sin, my need. I bring it all to the cross. And when the good news of God's love pours over me, it is then I realize, with my heart filled with *gratitude,* that Christ lives through me.

> No, I can't live the Christian life on my own—and he loves me anyway.

a cup of significance

I'm tired of being so...ordinary.

All my life I've sought to be extraordinary. I want to be admired by others and also admired by myself so that I don't feel the shame of being just plain ordinary.

I used to think that ambition was an indication of emotional health.

Not so. Extraordinary people feel extraordinary pressure to continue being extraordinary. It's a prison from which one cannot easily escape. The effort to maintain "extraordinary," to be a somebody, even to be a super Christian, takes so much energy and consumes all one's joy and peace. Worse, any of us who are bound to maintaining an extraordinary spiritual reputation eventually find Jesus oddly irrelevant, even an impediment, to one's purpose.

Jesus came to free us from the prison of needing to be extraordinary.

So I am free to be ordinary in him...
but that's not really ordinary at all.

a cup of abundance

I want more out of life.

I'm not proud to admit it, but I want more—more things, more success, more admirers, more influence, a better house, a newer car, a fresh idea, more productivity, more children, more spiritual growth… It's a very long list. *More* is what the world's about: having, doing, being *more* determines my value, and not just in others' eyes. I measure myself by more or less, and *more* is usually better. A man asked a friend how much money his family needed. He answered, "More." The pastor asked me about my commitment to Bible reading. I told him I was doing "more."

But *more* is a heavy load—one that shows me how little I trust God, how little I think I need him. *More's* actually a brilliant strategy of the Enemy.

The truth is, Jesus is not enough for me. I'm often fooled into thinking: Jesus + something more = contentment. What I need to do is pause and pray. Asking the Spirit to show me how much *more* rules my day begins the journey to plenty by taking away my desire for *more* and filling my heart with Jesus.

"I came that they may have life, and have it abundantly," he said (John 10:10).

Life in Jesus Christ is more than
I could ever need.

a cup of dependence

I'm desperate for God to help me run my life.

Most of us want a helper, someone to lean on, to turn to; we want a boost from a copilot. That makes most of us insane, really, because sane people don't want God as their *co*pilot. Insane people do because that makes them the pilot and they can have the advantages of his help without the disadvantage of giving up the controls.

We like the whole idea of God working for us. Maybe that's why we're generally impotent in our faith, saltless, fruitless with the lost, and dismissed by the watching world. Maybe that's why we're frustrated, grasping, angry, and weary. Maybe that's why others jump out our doors every chance they get!

Sanity really is better. When we're sane—when we let God be our pilot—we're inviting, welcoming to the watching world, relaxed, easy to be around.

What if we were flight attendants instead of copilots?

Imagine how joyful life could be, how safe, even fun, to serve others while God flies the plane across deep seas, above dry lands, over wicked wilderness (Psalm 107:23–43).

Life is so much better with
Jesus in command.

a cup of un-knowing

Suffering in the world makes me wonder about God, even doubt him.

What kind of God allows oppression, slaughter, injustice, floods, and famines? And why does he? Is he helpless? Does he care?

Cynics claim that suffering proves that God doesn't exist or that he's not loving. The truth is, no human has answers for such questions. Suffering is a mystery. And maybe we should learn to accept that.

After all, there is another mystery in all this, a comforting one that cynics cannot dismiss: the fact that love is everywhere suffering is. Watch a firefighter or a police officer or an AIDS volunteer. Watch a nurse hold a child's hand. The list goes on.

Love would not be natural to a random universe. It's intentional. Divine. So, despite all the many things we don't like or understand, there's comfort in seeing how love surrounds us, for if love surrounds us, God surrounds us.

No, I don't have to be able to explain everything; mystery is a reality of life that I'm invited to accept. The old Beatles song says it well.

Especially in the mystery of suffering, "Love is all we need."

a cup of freedom

I'm afraid of what others think of me.

It's bondage, this dependence on others' opinions, and it affects even my own opinion of myself.

I can tell because when I'm embarrassed, I lose my joy and peace.

How do I feel when I give the wrong answer, regret something I say, or hate the way my kids behave or the way I look when caught by surprise?

Well, if I want to either hide in a corner or tear someone's head off, I'm probably living in bondage to the expectations of others.

Have you been there too?

Probably. Most of us have. But do we have to stay there? One of the many kind things God does for us is to gently remind us that we sometimes forget how much he loves us just the way we are.

> He loves me even when
> I've said something dumb,
> lost control of the kids,
> or had a bad hair day.

a cup of comfort

Is my suffering God's punishment for my sin?

A pastor told my friend that her little girl's illness was probably God's judgment on family sin. And then he said that such sins had disqualified the family's prayers.

Imagine if you had been told that. Maybe you have—such condemnation is a common millstone hung around the necks of desperate Christians everywhere.

The truth is, our sins are washed away. All of them. Past. Present. Future. Our sins are out of the equation, put "as far as the east is from the west" (Psalm 103:12); they are paid for in full by Jesus.

Otherwise Jesus has died in vain. God's "chastening" (or "discipline," a favorite word among spiritual abusers) is not punishment but rather instruction. Do any of us pray from sinless hearts? Without Jesus, are any of us "qualified" to offer a single word to heaven?

No. But God turns toward sinners on bended knees—not away from them. Sure, God can use suffering to set us free from the chains that bind us. The point is made clear in James 1. And yes, sometimes it takes a hammer to break a chain. But that should never be confused with some ugly notion of penalty.

God is our Father, not our accuser.

a cup of easy

Rules are such a heavy burden.

I struggle with rules. Keeping them is exhausting. And I have trouble keeping them all straight anyway. Now, don't get me wrong. Straying from Jesus's way is not a good thing, but rule keeping is so often just plain legalism—the reliance on external obedience—and that's not the way of the cross.

Actually, legalism is a great way for many of us to duck the truth about ourselves. Keeping busy doing it all "right" keeps us from facing the darkness of our hearts. And focusing on rule keeping also helps us avoid paying any attention to the needs of others.

If we're exhausted by anything, it's because we've been led away from Jesus somewhere on our journey. Jesus offers us a better way; he wants to show us our hearts so that we may abandon ourselves and our obsessions, even the ones that look good. Yes, of course Jesus wants us to live according to his purposes—purposes designed for our welfare and the welfare of others. But his way should not be exhausting at all.

Rules can weigh us down,
but Jesus's yoke is light as a feather.

a cup of self-control

What's with my temper?!?

It's my new self-reliance detector. It's loud, and everybody notices when it goes off. Lately I've discovered that it usually boils over because I'm not being very Christ-reliant. You probably have a detector of your own. Maybe it's detachment, substance abuse, anxiety. Maybe even blood pressure or headaches.

Relying on self seduces us away from the sufficiency of God's grace in our lives. It tricks us into constructing false notions of God and ultimately leaves us desperately unsatisfied.

But we've been offered a different way to live. We've been made free to rely on Christ instead of on our own selves; we are called to a life of faith, and lives of faith don't have so many temper tantrums or escape-capades. Some even have fewer headaches and ulcers.

So what about a faith detector? How about hopeful smiles or kind words, calm answers or Self-less tears?

Faith detectors are easy to spot in others, and with an honest heart opened for God's grace, you'll see them in yourself too. Why not?

Self-control is a gift we can ask for.

Can you taste the fruit of the Spirit,
just waiting to be enjoyed?

a cup of identity

*Besetting sins make me feel like I'm not
a real Christian.*

A real Christian wouldn't sin so much, I think. *A real Christian would
have conquered lasting temptations.*

Sin's never a good thing. By definition, it hurts us and others. So
when we're stuck in a pattern of sin, bad things are regularly happening to someone.

Does habitual sin need to define us, though?

No. And that's better news than we might first think. Besetting
sins certainly feel like a master…and that's precisely what Satan wants
us to think. Believing that lie will send us into obsessive self-effort; it
will sink us in depression by depriving us of our true identity.

We are not defined by our sins, even if it sometimes seems like
that. We are the princes and princesses of a King, adopted as sons and
daughters of God. We need to remind ourselves and each other that
nothing—not even besetting sins—can separate us from the love of
God (Romans 8:35–39).

> No matter what, as a Christian,
> I'm a child of the King.

a cup of appreciation

I wish I were more thankful.

I'm afraid I've not been very appreciative. I'm too often disappointed by life. But even when life does go my way, I'm not particularly thankful because...honestly? I think I'm deserving.

I'm not happy about this. Once I prayed for a more thankful heart. Then everything went badly. After things went badly, I was stronger—and that made me thankful. So I'm learning about appreciation.

I've started asking the Spirit to show me all the good the Lord has done for me—in spite of myself. Then I can practice thanking God for allowing trouble in my life. I'm beginning to thank him for the disappointments and frustrations and even the tragedies that come my way, because I'm beginning to believe that he will make good things come of them (Romans 8:28).

Now, he needs to give me the faith to believe, and as he does, I'm actually seeing that what he has allowed in my life is exactly what I need. If I think about it, I'm thankful that I've realized that I'm not very thankful...which, ironically, I do appreciate!

> No, I can't make myself more
> appreciative, but he can.

a cup of honesty

I try so hard to feel great about myself.

I love being more gracious than others. It makes me feel better than them, even superior…and I love feeling superior. Being the best at good things feels nice, especially when I'm the best at being Christ-like. So I act like I'm forgiving others more quickly than my friends can, and I'm the first to welcome a guest at church and the first in the circle to pray. These are attempts to be a super Christian, a notch above other Christians.

But when I compare my graciousness to Jesus's instead of others', I'm exposed as the less-than-gracious person I really am.

It's good to be exposed, good to get fresh glimpses of my heart, because that's when I'm finally ready to run to my Father in heaven and confess the truth about myself.

The fact is that I'm not a super anything, especially not a super Christian. Hmm. Just saying that feels pretty good. Actually, it feels great to know that I can be honest about who I really am and still be loved by God. After all, he "knows our frame; He is mindful that we are but dust.… But the lovingkindness of the LORD is from ever-lasting to everlasting" (Psalm 103:14, 17).

It's good to see my heart because that helps to set me free.

a cup of security

Life scares me. Death terrifies me.

Why shouldn't I be shaky and afraid? We weren't created to live this twisted way of life. We weren't supposed to ever die. Thanks a lot, Adam and Eve. Nice job.

So, maybe it's okay for me not to feel so guilty about my fear. It's only natural. But must I live in fear?

No, the gospel gives me security in both life and death by telling me the good news that God keeps me safe on a foundation of love supported by immovable pillars. One pillar is Jesus's perfect life, which has satisfied the Father's desire for holiness. The second pillar is Jesus's death, which has satisfied the Father's demand for justice. Both Jesus's life and death have been given to me freely. That means I am in him in life (Galatians 2:20) and in him in death (Romans 6:4–5), and "we shall also be in the likeness of His resurrection" (Romans 6:5).

Lord, help me feel the truth of my security in you and your promises so that life will not scare me, nor death terrify me, so much as they do today. Thank you for holding my hand.

I am safe upon immovable pillars of love.

a cup of clinging

Self-confidence is my drug of choice.

It's another of my addictions really. Self-confidence fills me up, makes me feel strong, secure, invincible; it keeps me from thinking I need Jesus, makes prayer a bother…like the Bible. It leaves me pretty sure that I don't need God and that I certainly don't need others. Duty, obedience, goals, and hard work become the fuel for my daily motivation. Through everything, self-confidence remains my drug of choice even though it's as dangerous—maybe more dangerous—to me than a drink is to an alcoholic.

I need Jesus's help. I need his mercy. I'm unable to shake this addiction on my own. I need him to take me to the I-don't-have-the-answers-anymore place of trust and dependence so I'll be sane, so I can rest. When I'm secretly feeling weak, needy, fearful, discouraged, or frustrated and have more desperateness in my life, I abandon my self-confidence and cling to Christ, even as he has been clinging to me all along. That's when I rediscover the joy of my faith. That's when I'm really free.

I may be desperate for self-confidence, but real desperation leads me to the joy of letting go of self.

a cup of humility

I just keep believing the lie.

Each day I'm suckered into believing the same lie that my great-great-great-great-great-grandparents Adam and Eve got suckered into believing: that I can function independently of God (Genesis 3). This translates into imagining that I have wisdom worth leaning on, the knowledge of what's best for me, the ability to make my life happy, the power to rule others, and on and on.

Adam and Eve were the first control freaks, and autonomy was the forbidden fruit that they really wanted. But are we, their descendants, really any different?

Well, no, not at all. We yield to that same temptation every day. That's why prayer is not central to our lives. That's why we go crazy trying to run our lives and everyone's around us. We really do want to be like God in so many terrible ways. We may think we want to be like God, but the trying takes a toll.

Lord, forgive me for wanting to believe the lie. Set me free from the tyranny of self-rule, and restore me to the innocence of a dependent child once again. Help me believe what the psalmist said (Psalm 100:3): that you are God, that you made me and not I myself.

Thank God, I don't have to try being a little god anymore.

a cup of quiet

I can't turn off my brain.

I find myself always thinking, planning, sorting, analyzing, rethinking. On vacation, brushing my teeth, wherever—my mind never stops.

I have to admit to myself that I think a lot because I have a constant fear of not getting something right, of not performing well. My mind constantly mulls over today, tomorrow, next week.

But nonstop thinking and analyzing can be overrated, a way of tricking myself into believing I can control my world. I need to remember that I'm not really in charge of my life. I need to choose to believe Psalm 46:10 and stop thinking from time to time and just rest my brain.

> How good it is to be still and
> know that he is God.

a cup of
righteousness

Needing to be right is a terrible burden.

Being right is what's most important to me most of the time, especially being right about spiritual things, but also about nearly everything else. I *need* to be right. My confidence depends on it, my reputation rests on it, my happiness feeds on it. So my opinions are held stubbornly. I declare them, loudly. I want—no—I demand that others agree with me.

Being right gives me life.

Or so I've too often thought. When I'm honest, though, what I'm really fighting for is my own *right*eousness. I can barely breathe without feeling *right*eous. I yearn so desperately to be *right*eous, yet only he is.

Truly, the Scripture says (Romans 3:10), "there is none righteous, not even one"…and that means me too.

Guess what? In a weird way, that's a relief to admit. Being "right" all the time is just too hard. *Thank you, Jesus.*

> I am free from being right because
> Jesus already is.

a cup of faith

Please help me find more faith.

That, like confusion, is one of the things I have in common with Jesus's head-scratching disciples. I try hard to muster faith, but it just doesn't come to me…and I have a hunch most of us are a little low on the faith meter.

I was walking past some old folks in a home who were singing an old hymn at the end of their lunch. I paused to listen, jealous of the earnestness in their voices, and then I was stopped by the last line:

> Jesus, Jesus, precious Jesus!
> O for grace to trust him more.

How that hit me. Jesus is more than the object of our faith; he's also the source of it.

No amount of my striving will create more faith in my heart. My part is to confess my self-reliance. His pleasure is to give me faith as a free, unearned gift of love, just like it says in Ephesians 2:8: "For by grace you have been saved through faith; and that not of yourselves, it is the gift of God."

I don't have to muster up more faith—
faith is a gift from God.

a cup of adoption

I'm often ashamed of who I am.

The interesting thing is, though, that no one could ever shame us—we couldn't even shame ourselves—if our self-esteem wasn't more precious to us than Jesus. It's impossible for us to feel foolish, embarrassed, or humiliated unless we forget that our names are written in heaven.

Once I wore mismatched shoes to a speaking engagement. I saw some people giggling in the audience, and when I looked down my eyes locked on one brown shoe and one black shoe. I never wanted to look up.

Of course we all have those kinds of awful moments in life, moments we feel stupid. Why not? Sometimes we *are* stupid!

But what if we were to die to our self-esteem? What if we asked God to remind us of the wonder of our adoption? Shame would lose its power to dominate us, and in its place would come the courage and confidence befitting our true identity as the sons and daughters of the Creator.

> When I remember who I really am,
> shame goes away.

a cup of focus

Morality is a terrible struggle.

Really, it's my obsession: I'm becoming more and more perfection-istic, judgmental, critical, intense, uptight, and nervous. I have trouble loving others because I'm obsessed with my behavior—and theirs. I look around at church and see lots of other hard, unhappy, unwelcoming, defensive faces.

Something's very wrong.

Living morally is a good thing, of course. It's the way God protects us and others from terrible things. But obsession with anything except Jesus is not a good thing. In fact, worshiping morality instead of Jesus is idolatry. When I'm consumed with my moral performance and find myself obsessively evaluating the morality of others, I've become a believer in moralism, not the gospel.

My attention to morals is important but, ah, the gospel is something else entirely. The gospel teaches me that sound living is the natural fruit of a relationship with God—that the focus of faith is Jesus, not behavior. When I learn to love Jesus, I'll want to live his way (John 14:15), and I'll be freed from the religion of moralism and transformed into a lover of others.

When I keep my eyes on Jesus,
right living happens.

a cup of love

Sometimes I hate myself.

I see so many situations where I believe I could have done better. This leaves me angry with myself, sometimes shattered to the point of self-hatred.

Oddly, this self-contempt is really pride: I'm despising myself because I believe I could have done better. (See what I mean? Pride.) I may hate myself for failing, but I'm never humbled. In this strange way, my pride keeps me in bondage to my self-contempt; it's a hard way to live.

I need to remember that Jesus isn't feeling the same way about me that I feel about me. He knows very well what I often don't like to admit—that I am a limited human being. And guess what? He loves me anyway.

When I get a glimpse of myself as Jesus sees me, I find it easier to accept my limitations. I can confess my pride with tears of thankfulness for his unfailing love. That's when I'm suddenly happy to let go of my self-contempt. It feels so good to know that he doesn't despise me even when I despise myself. And more (Romans 8:35–39), it's not just that he doesn't despise me, but he actually does treasure me!

How good to know that Jesus loves me
even when I despise myself.

a cup of forgiveness

Admitting weakness is so hard for me to do.

When I was eight, I surveyed a grocer's shelf and decided to steal a package of salted pumpkin seeds. (Yes, I passed over baseball cards and candy and went for salted pumpkin seeds.) Once outside, I opened the package and found the snack to be, well, too salty and a bit boring. But then came the guilt and the terror. I realized I was a thief and hid behind a bush, nervous, fearful, paranoid—certain the whole world knew what I'd done. I said the word *thief* to myself, and it tasted worse than the pumpkin seeds. My world felt so heavy.

So I took a breath and walked back to the store, where I handed the owner his half-eaten package with a confession. He forgave me and the world felt lighter.

Admitting sin, weakness, and failure is the pathway to wholeness. A kind and gracious thing the Spirit does for me is to freshly convict me of my sin so that I can be freshly in love with Jesus and others, especially the lost. Naming sin, calling it what it is with specificity, is like dropping a terrible weight from our shoulders (1 John 1:9).

> Confession is the way of happiness because it allows us to taste grace.

a cup of mystery

I'm so tired of trying to figure out God.

I like mysteries, except mysteries about God. I think this is because of two things. First, people tell me I'm supposed to understand God—that it's my job and that's how the relationship works. Second, a little voice inside tells me that if I can figure out God, then I can control him.

So I obsess over theology; I read Scripture for the purpose of understanding every word, and then I fight for my opinions.

But I'm wasting my time. God is a mystery. Who can know the mind of God (Romans 11:34)? I think God likes being a mystery. I'm invited to love him without understanding him. And who do I think I am imagining that I could ever understand him? I am so arrogant. God is not about to be controlled by me. What I know of him is exactly what he wants me to know. No more. No less.

This is kind of a relief. It's liberating to allow for mystery. It means I can stop the impossible task of having to figure it all out. Of course, it also means I have to accept the idea that I'll never control God. In my saner moments, that's good news. Allowing for mystery allows for possibilities, lets me relax, allows me to trust him more.

> What a relief to know that
> I don't have to understand him
> in order to be loved by him.

a cup of un-control

Life feels so heavy.

If I'm feeling weighed down, it may be because I've declared myself CEO of my life. Actually, I probably believe that I need control more than I need Jesus. I haven't said those words to anyone else, and they're hard to admit to myself. But my joy-less, peace-less, exhausting existence makes it pretty clear that I've decided to bear the responsibility of running my life.

Of course, I mouth the words that God's the boss, but I know I don't believe that—not really, at least not most of the time. The proof is in my anxiety and anger, my frustration and secret fears. The fact is that I live most of my Christian life without the benefit of Christ.

However, I've been told that I really can retire. No, better than that. I'm told that I can just quit and give the position of CEO and all its problems to Jesus.

Sounds like good news to me. And I have a hunch that my shareholders—my sofa-jockey spouse, my eye-rolling kids, my arms-folded, toe-tapping friends—would be delighted.

Life can be freer with Jesus
as CEO of my life.

a cup of
Christ-esteem

I worry constantly about my reputation.

I suppose we all care an awful lot about what others think of us. And we spend a lot of time wondering about it. We evaluate a certain look someone casts our way; we worry about a comment. We go to great lengths to keep people imagining us to be the way we want them to see us. Even (or maybe especially) at church, we get awfully self-conscious of what others are thinking.

But I find reputation maintenance to be hard work. Why can't I be content with what the Father of the universe thinks about me? Surely I am my Father's true love. So I don't need to minimize, rationalize, or deny my faults and weaknesses or sins to him, because they're not issues for him. I don't need to maintain a reputation with him, because my image is within Christ's, and Christ's reputation is just fine.

> How good to be free to love others
> without worrying one bit about
> what anyone thinks of me.

a cup of weakness

I just can't admit my weaknesses.

But how could things in my life (and others') be different if I did admit my failings and shortcomings?

Maybe I'd…

- feel less pressure, fear, frustration, and discouragement
- live and work with reckless abandon, even boldness
- liberate my talents
- speak honestly and offer balanced thinking to others
- celebrate joy
- love others and myself

It's amazing how admitting weakness strengthens me.

a cup of trust

It's so hard to trust in Jesus.

When I was a little kid, I trusted him. Easily.

Since then too many people have tried to show me a different Jesus: the angry Judge, the "I'd better not catch you doing that at the Second Coming" Son of God. Isn't he the one who kills you if you take communion "unworthily"? Doesn't that Jesus keep a record of every one of my sins so he can nail me at the Judgment?

What happened to the Jesus of the Sunday school flannel board? The one who defended the weak, the friend of sinners, the healer of the sick, the comforter to the grieving? What happened to the Jesus who threw injustice, greed, and religious abuse out of his Father's house?

That's the Jesus I need to know again. That's the Jesus I want to see and trust (Philippians 3:10).

> Thank goodness for a Jesus more trustworthy than I can ever know.

a cup of others

I don't love others well.

One of the reasons is that I'm desperate to *be* loved. I don't know anyone who loves me unless I've performed well…and, frankly, I find no end to the performance that's expected.

So where do I find the power to love others?

By first being unconditionally loved.

Who loves me that way?

Jesus.

By reminding myself every day of his love for me, I can be less and less desperate. As my awareness of his love fills me, love for others will come with less and less effort, without resentment, anger, or conditions of my own (1 John 4).

> Yes, I can more easily love others—
> and love them well—the more
> I understand how much
> he first loved me.

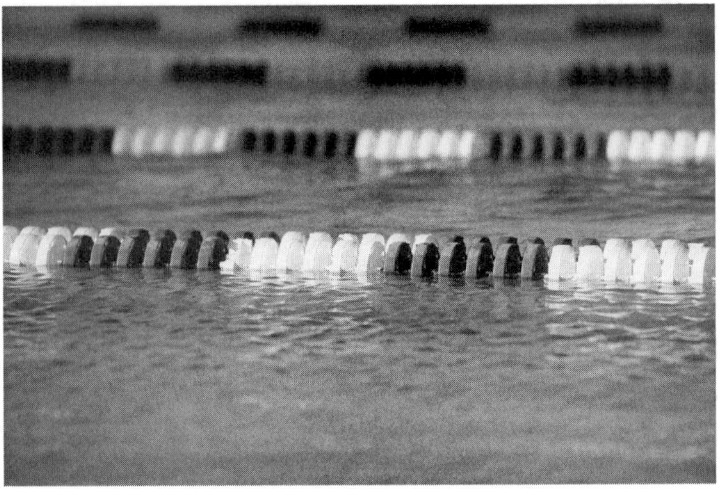

a cup of possibility

My days feel impossible.

The truth is that this day really will be impossible to handle...without Jesus. Yet Satan wants me to believe that I've been equipped to do just fine. He wants me thinking that the spiritual muscle-building books I read and the self-inflation steroids I get from Christian radio have provided the formulas I need.

Why do I allow these things to tempt me into the delicious delusion that my day—no, my whole Christian life—is doable if I would just bench-press Jesus a little harder?

I've come to know better.

The more I'm deluded into believing that I'm spiritually competent, the less likely my day will include Jesus at all. And that really will make for an impossible day.

So I'm trying to resist the flexing. Instead I'm focusing my exercise on the hardest spiritual muscle-builder of all: deep knee bending...to pray. Getting on my knees to him—and him alone—makes all the difference (Mark 10:27 and Philippians 4:13).

Yes, my day is impossible without Jesus,
but *in* him, all things are possible.

a cup of hope

Living the way I do must be abnormal.

I do the things I don't want to do. And I don't do the things I want to do. That's the sad reality of my life.

Am I a normal Christian?

Well, yes. Romans 7, in a strange way, offers a message of comfort—not permission for me to feel good about my limitations, but affirmation that I'm not abnormal, not alone. The apostle Paul makes it very clear that this struggle with the things done and the things left undone has been his too. He even claimed to be the chief of all sinners (1 Timothy 1:15).

So where's the good news?

In Romans 8:1.

In spite of our "normal" condition, "there is now no condemnation for those who are in Christ Jesus."

a cup of glad

I want so desperately to be happy.

When I'm honest, I admit that I think happiness should be the point of living.

Happiness eludes me, though, and somewhere inside I know that I can't make myself happy. But there are times that I do try: when I'm confident, intense, opinionated, in a hurry. I foolishly operate like a Lone Ranger trying to deny the weight of the world on my shoulders. That's when I'm clueless as to my need of a Savior to take me by the hand and lead me into whatever he thinks is best for me.

Funny thing is, the harder I try being happy, the less happy I actually am.

So when the Holy Spirit convicts me of my need for him to be the source of all joy, I find that I'm content to be the clueless, child-like, weak, needy, adopted orphan of the Most High God once again. That's when it's fun to be a Christian. That's when I'm free to face life—with or without happiness—because life can be so much better when I'm content to be clueless.

Happy? Not always. Glad hearted?
Absolutely.

a cup of tomorrow

I don't like being such a needy person.

The voices in and around me urge me to think that my biggest need is for the nagging problems in my life to be solved. More money, more fun, a better reputation, more of this, better of that…these are what the voices say I need. And they are powerful voices.

So how do I shut out the voices?

I can allow myself to feel overwhelmed that my name is written in heaven. I can ask the Spirit to show me the truth about my heart and desires, to give me a glimpse of heaven as Isaiah experienced (Isaiah 6).

When the Spirit fills my imagination with images of my eternal home, things sure look different here. Everything else pales by comparison. What's so important here when the glories of heaven are waiting for me?

Of course, I live in the here and now.

But seeing heaven in my future puts all my nows in perspective.

a cup of amazing

I am desperate for God's favor.

I work hard to please him, and I admit that I feel good about myself when I think I've earned God's pleasure. In fact, I often believe that God owes me a bonus for all the good I've done!

All the effort is tiring, though. I'm worn out, and I spend a lot of time counting off what I think God owes me. I hope he pays overtime. And, by the way, I can't stand thinking that he gives his favor to some people as a gift. That makes all my work look stupid.

But something smells fishy about this. Winning his favor (and dodging his anger) makes my relationship with God about me. It's as if the real object of my service is the blessings and not him. Somehow my life has become a matter of manipulating God to reward me…to love me more and not punish me.

I know that sounds quite horrible.

The wonderful truth is that I really can't make him love me any more than he already does. No matter how many church functions I organize, how many missionaries I support, or how good I am to others, he just keeps on loving me…just the same.

Nothing I do or don't do changes the
way God feels about me.

a cup of excitement

Jesus sometimes bores me.

Oh, sure, I'm glad he's letting me into heaven, but beyond that, I'm not very excited. I'm easily bored by the Bible, prayer, church, and, frankly, even the plight of the lost.

Why is that?

Those of us who won't look honestly at ourselves are left with a sense of being forgiven little. Subsequently, small sinners need only small saviors. We have no joy in the wonder of God's grace, and we are utterly incapable of loving others.

That's why taking a hard, honest look at ourselves can be a good thing. Though often painful, seeing opens our eyes to the good news about the vast love of Jesus. Asking the Holy Spirit to show us how very much we've been forgiven will move us to our knees in gratitude, then to our feet in celebration.

Understanding how much I've been forgiven helps me find Jesus to be huge in my life: important, relevant, and exciting.

Big sinner = big Savior + big joy!

a cup of safety

I have trust issues.

Everyone has let me down at one time or another. Even God.

He often doesn't do what I expect him to, so I have trouble trusting him. I'm actually afraid of him. He just doesn't feel safe. No one does.

It's hard to live without trusting. To make matters worse, I can't admit this to anyone because I can't trust them to know me that well. If they did, they wouldn't trust me! And do you have any idea what they could do to me if they really knew me?

I already feel better admitting this to myself, though. I'm pretty sure that's all I can do, except…maybe I should pray. Maybe if I admit to God that he scares me too much for me to trust him, then he will answer me.

He answered a similar prayer of David's in the Bible. David said, "But when [I] cried to Him for help, He heard" (Psalm 22:24 and 28:6–7).

Yes, I may always have trust issues,
but God hears and helps.

a cup of opportunity

Will problems never cease!

No. And they come at me every day. Problems on the job, with my kids, spouse, friends, health, money, relatives, and IN-LAWS (the worst)!

But maybe my problems don't have to hinder a joy-filled life. After all, don't my problems nudge me to go to Jesus, to know him better? Don't problems wake me from comfort and ease, quicken my faith, bring me back to God and his promise that "all things…work together for good" (Romans 8:28)?

True, I don't want problems. I'm not completely nuts. But when problems come, as they inevitably do, I'm learning to say "thank you" before I start complaining.

> Problems will always be part of life, but I'm grateful they open the door to hope.

a cup of strength

I want so badly to feel strong.

Ironically, my strength is my weakness. If the Enemy can trick me into leaning on my own power, I'm deceived as to the reality of my need of a Savior. When I rely on myself, I have little need of intimacy with Jesus, little need of grace, little need of fresh conviction of sin…and a great need for things to go my way. That's why Paul said in 2 Corinthians 12:9, "Most gladly, therefore, I will rather boast about my weaknesses, so that the power of Christ may dwell in me."

Our churches often urge Christians to be strong. That's why so many don't feel safe or loved, why few are approachable. We're all busy flexing.

I once was asked the single word that best describes a Christian, and I answered, "Obedient." But this wasn't the desired answer, so I tried again: "Okay, how about strong? victorious? overcoming?"

The person who asked the question shook his head. "Weak is what we really are," he said, looking me in the eye with a smile, "and we have great power in our weakness."

Wow.

> My weakness is my strength
> because Jesus lives in me—
> and he's not weak at all.

a cup of all's well

Complaining drives me nuts.

Yet I do it all the time. My spouse gets tired of it; my kids turn away. I'm pretty sure it's a problem. Of course, I really get tired of other people's complaints.

When complaining characterizes my life, I'm worshiping an idol, not Jesus. When nothing my kids, spouse, or friends do pleases me, when everything frustrates my agenda and expectations, then I can be pretty sure I'm worshiping the idol of "I."

The great "I" claims to know what, when, and how things should be. And when things are not the way the mighty "I" wants, "I" worshipers complain. Loudly. To everyone. That's how you spot an "I" worshiper.

When thanksgiving characterizes my life, I know my heart is closer to Jesus. How else could I face the imperfection all around me with a smile and a steady eye? Wouldn't it be so nice to complain less and smile more?

> In Christ I have a reason to smile in the face of frustration and disappointment.

a cup of good fruit

I really am self-absorbed.

The fruit of self—whether self-accomplishment, self-righteousness, self-glory, or self-consciousness—is eventual insanity, as I become more and more intense, self-centered, anxious, and unapproachable.

But a focus on Jesus-accomplishment, Jesus-righteousness, Jesus-glory, and Jesus-consciousness leads to sanity—joy and peace regardless of everything else going on around me. Such a shift in focus lets me and those around me enjoy the fruit of the Spirit named in Galatians 5: love, joy, peace, patience, kindness, goodness, faithfulness, gentleness, self-control. And guess what? It lets me enjoy that good fruit too.

So how do I focus more on Jesus instead of myself?

A good place to start is by asking the Spirit to whisper in my ear every time I'm worried about my performance, evaluating my reputation, or criticizing or applauding myself.

When I stop caring about my anything,
then I'll be free.

a cup of plenty

Jesus is not enough for me.

His grace, his righteousness, even his daily presence don't seem like enough to make me happy. I want something more, like being a somebody in the eyes of others and in my own eyes. I want to feel good about my obedience and spiritual growth, my successful marriage, business, looks, and, yes, even my ministry. I want to be recognized.

I don't like depending on Jesus. I know that sounds terrible, but it's true.

How I long for the freedom to be a nobody like the whore in Luke 7 for whom Jesus and his righteousness were enough. Imagine living like the old hymn says, "My hope is built on nothing less than Jesus's blood and righteousness."

Why have I tried to build my life on more than Jesus's blood and righteousness?

Maybe if I could see myself as Jesus does—as the forgiven sinner—I might not be so quick to look past him. I need the Spirit to teach me the truth that I am a far greater sinner than I could ever imagine, and yet Jesus loves me more than I will ever know.

With my Self put in place, Jesus becomes more than enough.

a cup of surprise

I've given up trying to determine how I can change spiritually.

If I try to grow spiritually, I find the exercise futile. But when I give up the trying and put my attention on God's grace through his amazing love, I soon find surprising changes in my life:

- I don't know the answer to something, and that's okay.
- I'm curious and expectant about the future.
- I'm joyful and peaceful in hard situations.
- I'm not stressed even though I have a lot to do.
- I'm thankful in the midst of circumstances for which no reasonable person would be thankful.
- Things are normal, but it dawns on me to pray anyway.
- I have a fresh sense of having been forgiven much.

The best surprise?

> How grateful I am that the Spirit changes me when I'm not even looking.

a cup of air

Life's so heavy I can't breathe.

Yet Jesus offers me his yoke, light as a feather (Matthew 11:30), in exchange for my own burdensome one. Life would look very different with a lighter yoke, wouldn't it? I could throw back my shoulders and breathe deeply.

If I would only learn to carry Jesus's yoke into a problem, I wouldn't be making decisions on my own; I'd ask him. And I'd feel far less pressure, discouragement, fear, and frustration. It would be a great way to live.

Of course, can any of us honestly say we live that way? Not me. But when I start complaining that my burdens are heavy and my yoke is hard to bear, I can be pretty sure it is *my* burden and *my* yoke that I'm carrying.

The problem is, I can't lift my own burdens off my back in my own strength. I need the Holy Spirit to lift them away because they're far too heavy for me to lift off myself. Nor can I just go grab Jesus's yoke and put in around my neck. He wants to do that for me. So why don't I start praying that way?

> Jesus makes the crosses I bear light
> because he carries them for me.

a cup of waiting

God seems silent in my life.

Others seem to have their prayers answered. Not me, not unless all of my prayers are being answered with a disinterested no.

Hmm. So does that mean others have more faith? Are they more obedient, more in touch with God, more favored by him, than I am? Seems logical; certainly feels that way.

But what about Jesus on the cross? Through all his anguish the Father remained silent. Yet Jesus was faithful. He was obedient "to the point of death" (Philippians 2:8). He was in touch with God and certainly favored.

Maybe I've confused God's silence with neglect. Maybe his silence isn't a bored dismissal of me, but a carefully considered, patient, perhaps even painful rejection of my desires in favor of my welfare. Maybe I just need to wait.

I think I'm onto something here, something good. For I know that not even a sparrow falls to the ground without God knowing (Matthew 10:29), and Jesus says I am more loved than the sparrows. So although it may seem like God's not listening, I can ask him to teach me how to fasten my hopes on his Word. The fact is, the Lord hears when I call to him (Psalm 4:3).

Sometimes faith is more a matter
of believing than feeling.

a cup of liberation

I'm addicted to my ideas of Christianity.
I love my "victorious" living.

I imitate the virtues of Christianity, like kindness and patience and self-control, better than most. I can't get enough ministry. I've filled my bookshelves with Christian books. I love how much I read my Bible. I pray without ceasing. I listen to Christian music and have a fish sign on my car. I can even say the words *fellowship* and *testimony* in front of my non-Christian friends without embarrassment. And I'm a good witness in all I do.

See how I just love my Christianity?

The problem is that I don't love Jesus all that much. Not really. I'd rather love the things *about* him rather than *him*. Religion is easier than relationship with him.

And yet…religion isn't working.

Father, forgive me for robbing you. Have mercy on one who would steal your Son's image for himself. Set me free from my idea of Christianity so that I may love Jesus instead.

I'm grateful Jesus still loves addicts,
even religious ones.

a cup of clarity

Denial tries to rob me.

I hang around with Denial a lot. He keeps me blind to the truth about myself. Whenever we're together, I become competitive, intense, joyless, and angry. And why not? When I'm blind, I begin to imagine the self to be far more than it is. Denial is like that.

If you haven't noticed, Denial and the Holy Spirit don't get along. The Spirit wants me to see clearly; he wants me to understand my weaknesses and failures, my sin and desperate neediness, because that kind of vision sets me free to hide in him. Of course, sometimes sight is blinding; it hurts. But it doesn't hurt as much as Denial, and Denial hurts others too.

So when Denial goes away, I have hope, because the Spirit is also quick to show me how able he is to take care of me. That's when I'm okay accepting the truth about who I really am.

> Life is good when the
> truth sets me free.

a cup of secrets

I pretend to be humble.

You might think I'm humble, maybe even a good Christian, a shining star for Jesus.

The truth is, I'm so eaten up with my own glory, so insecure in myself, that I have no time for the glory of the Creator, the very One who extends grace to me in the most precious gift he has ever given anyone.

Yes, I'm afraid I know very well who I am. I'm filled with pride. I love accolades. I find self-glory to be delicious. And, yes, I'm secretly scared to death of losing the worship that I think I deserve. I fear being exposed as an inner weakling or doubter, a self-serving hypocrite. I've been secretly ashamed, and I wonder how long it will take you to find out.

Thanks be to God, who knows exactly who I am. Like Eve, we can't hide from God. And knowing that he knows what he knows astonishes me. It's like Colossians 3:12 says...

> In spite of all these things,
> he loves me and even calls me holy.

a cup of beloving

I wish I knew what today was about.

I'm tempted to believe that today's purpose is to complete some kind of checklist, to accomplish some goal, maybe even do something amazing for Jesus.

But the Bible's idea of today seems different—and pretty plain. John 6:29 says, "This is the work of God, that you believe in Him whom He has sent."

So today isn't about accomplishing things. It's about believing. But what is "believing," anyway?

Belief in Jesus has two parts: believing *about* and believing *in*. The first has to do with the mind, assenting to the facts about Jesus. But it's more than just believing *about,* because even Satan knows who Jesus is (James 2:19).

Maybe the other part is the key, the part about believing *in* and how that springs from the heart. It's like the Old English word *beloving*. Believing *in* Jesus really is *beloving* him, trusting him like a child trusts a parent, leaning into his arms in a relationship of confident, loving dependence. Beloving Jesus makes all the difference today.

> Thank goodness today is about
> Christ alone—beloving him and
> accepting his beloving of me.

a cup of release

Why am I so obsessed with obedience?

I try to obey all the time, and I usually feel great when I do.

Sometimes that's okay, but show me someone obsessed with obedience and I'll show you someone whose motivation is at least partly self-righteous.

I need to be careful about measuring things by the way they make me feel. Outward obedience is important, but it's not my biggest issue. The more pressing issue is my passion for independence from God, whether that's driven by outright rebellion or by the more subtle danger of self-righteousness. When driven by an obsession for obedience, I really need to question my motivation... because obeying is not always obedience.

True obedience comes from love; it flows out of gratitude for God's love. God doesn't want me to be a robotic, duty-bound, obsessive law keeper driven by some feel-good self-righteousness.

If I focus on gratitude to God instead of external behavior, obedience will spring from a glad heart set free from obsession.

a cup of the Spirit

I'm addicted to feeling superior.

My knee-jerk reaction to most of life is to position myself in such a way that I'm superior to somebody, anybody. So I look for the Achilles heel in others: how they dress, talk, walk, drive, decorate, invest, believe, and on and on. During a group picture, I always stand next to the short guy so I'll look taller. I wonder how that makes him feel.

Cognitively, I know better. I know that the way I'm supposed to view others is with selfless grace. Deep inside I really do want to be gracious instead of critical, always comparing, always holding court. But graciousness is not my natural tendency; it flies in the face of my addiction.

Now, sometimes I'm good at faking graciousness, like letting someone have the last piece of cake that I really didn't want anyway. But I only offer real grace when the Spirit is at work in me, humbling me. Those moments of genuine humility are so precious, so liberating, and so much better than my addiction.

> When I'm stripped of the Self within me—the one whispering to *do, be,* and *have* better than all the rest— then I'm free from my addiction.

a cup of who cares?

Success and failure are wearisome themes in my life.

I'm finding that success is overrated as a blessing and failure is overrated as a problem. Satan wants me consumed with the desire for success so he can blind me from the success I already have as an heir to God's kingdom. Satan also wants me tangled up in failure-avoidance so he can terrorize me, weird me out, inhibit me from operating with the zest of life that's a big benefit of walking intimately with Jesus.

Strangely, the more indifferent I am to success and failure, the more I operate comfortably, even with reckless abandon, and the more likely I am to make a real difference in the lives of others...differences that go far beyond my limiting notions of success and failure.

> When my eyes and thoughts are fixed on Jesus instead of on my performance, I can be indifferent to success and failure—and free to serve others.

a cup of courage

Fear is my shadow.

I fear for my children, my job, my marriage, my health, for my reputation and my life. I fear death. I fear God—and not in the good kind of way.

I can't make myself stop being afraid; I think I'm afraid because I don't believe.

Of course, I'm not alone. The first thing Adam and Eve experienced after they sinned was fear. (The second was shame, my other companion.) Even the apostle Peter was afraid. He was scared to death to walk on the water…even with Jesus standing there.

I don't want to be afraid, but I can't *not* be, not on my own.

So what can I do?

I can admit my fear to Jesus.

I can cry out like Peter did.

Admitting my fear is such a relief. I think it's a good beginning. After that, I'll need to ask the Holy Spirit to give me the faith to believe God's promise in 1 John 4:18:

> "There is no fear in love; but perfect love casts out fear."

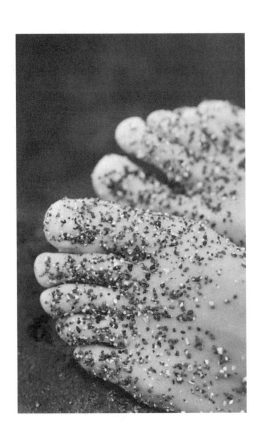

a cup of reality

Limitations bother me.

It's a good thing to accept the reality of my limitations. I know that statement flies in the face of nearly everything anyone's ever said to me, but I'm tired of denying the truth. Yes, I do have my limits. Face it, we all have them. This is part of being human.

God certainly knows and, frankly, even expects me to have limitations. The psalmist wrote, "For He Himself knows our frame; He is mindful that we are but dust" (Psalm 103:14). So if he knows my little secret anyway, wouldn't it just be easier to recognize my limitations and then name them? How about I get really crazy and thank him for leaving me deficient in spots so that I'll need him more!

Ah, accepting the truth of limitations is such a huge relief.

I know some folks will say I could use this as an excuse to fail. Well, my limitations are certainly reasons that I fail. Excuses? No. But why can't I offer myself—why can't we offer one another—the mercy that Jesus extends in simply acknowledging the truth about our limitations? That would be amazing grace indeed.

Limitations are part of a fallen world
in which Jesus loves anyway.

a cup of approval

Criticism is hard for me to take.

In fact, a core motivation in my life has been to avoid criticism. I despise the humiliation that follows criticism; it's driven my dysfunctional reaction to the many varied situations I face each day. I've bought uncomfortable clothes, hidden from certain people, agreed with others, eaten food that I hate, read really boring books, and bleached my teeth—all to avoid criticism. I've even parked blocks away from my destination because my car was dirty.

But I've learned that it's impossible to feel humiliated unless my self-esteem is more precious to me than Jesus. To the extent that I believe what Jesus thinks of me—that I am his beloved friend—I will care less about being criticized.

As I slowly die to my reputation, the shame of ridicule is emptied of its power. So go ahead, world! Criticize me, ridicule me, laugh at me, pity me, judge me, dismiss me, ignore me. Jesus loves me, this I know.

Jesus offers freedom from the power of Criticism and its ugly brother, Ridicule.

a cup of order

I must have order in my life.

Order is important to me—and that's actually something of an understatement. I spend my days fighting chaos and demanding order against all odds. Considering what I'm up against, I admit that the battle isn't easy. If you saw my wife's closet, you'd understand. And if you saw my calendar, if you knew the background expectations, the timetables, and the deadlines, you'd understand even more why order is a supreme goal of mine.

I try so hard to keep my world neat and tidy, just as I want—no—*need* it to be.

But the Author of order is God, not me; order is ultimately found in him, not in the way I organize life. I've come to learn (the hard way) that when I don't see order in my life, it doesn't mean it isn't there. It just means that things are in a different kind of order than I might prefer.

Even the chaos of my life is ordered by our Father in heaven, for he is a whirlwind too—a good whirlwind that allows the swirl of life to teach me to hang on tightly to Jesus. In the end, isn't that the real definition of order anyway?

God's mysterious order is present especially in the chaos of our lives.

a cup of truth

I worry about knowing the truth.

Most of us spend our lives trying to figure everything out; we're obsessed with getting things right. We've believed the lies of science that limit reality to the five senses, and we define *truth* as the sum of provable facts. So we conclude that if we get the facts straight, we have the truth.

This is an annoying attitude in others. Don't you just love a party with an opinionated bully demanding that everyone agree with him or her? Or how about your Bible study or Sunday school class—doesn't it feel intimidating when someone claims to have all the answers?

I'm afraid many of us have confused knowledge with truth.

But truth isn't only knowledge. Truth is a living person. Jesus Christ is truth (John 14:6).

That means I can stop wringing my hands, trembling at the thought that I might have missed something about the facts. I can afford to be wrong sometimes. I can let go of my death grip on opinions.

I can actually listen to another's insight...because the living Truth is doing just fine.

a cup of providence

All things don't seem to work together for good.

I know that's what Romans 8:28 says, but I'm not so sure sometimes. The last coherent words I ever heard my God-fearing grandmother say were "God is good." She said that on her way into brain surgery and then spent nine years anxiously staring at her room as a victim of brain damage. I remember visiting my grandfather, a faithful Bible-church pastor, in his personal care unit. He was disoriented and tied to his chair, slumping sideways. Above his head hung a cockeyed plaque of Romans 8:28. I remember shaking my head while straightening the plaque.

Yes, I know the Romans passage that explains "good" is our being conformed to Christ's image and all that. Yes, I get it. But, honestly, none of that makes me feel any better.

I suppose it's fortunate that I don't have to understand or believe what God says for it to be true. Nor does it matter if I approve of how he governs this world. God will be God. I don't understand his ways, but I do know that I, like my grandparents, am his beloved child. He loves me no less.

Even when I shake my fist in bitter confusion, God holds me close and uses my anger for my ultimate good.

a cup of letting go

I clutch desperately to my sense of self-worth.

Our culture wants me to feel so good about my Self. Advertisers know this well. Their messages are subtle, but they touch our natural desire to feel good about who we are, quite apart from Jesus.

I know I'm created in the image of God and, yes, I should appreciate the dignity that's mine as his child. Every human being has great worth. But that's very different from the kind of self-worth that has warped into self-worship.

So how do I know if I'm expressing godly self-respect or simply filled with ego-idolatry?

I can get a clue when things don't go my way and I lose my joy and peace. I can figure I'm worshiping my Self when I'm bored with the Bible, bored with church, bored with Jesus; when I fail to think of others first…or even at all; when I'm easily angered and often frustrated; when I'm unapproachable, uncompassionate, and unforgiving.

Self-respect has its place, but looking to serve it instead of God is such a waste of life. Why don't I just turn my eyes upon Jesus, just like the old song says?

Truly, "the things of earth will grow strangely dim in the light of his glory and grace."

a cup of defiance

I'm not going to take it anymore.

I'm pretty tired of good Christians hammering me for my sins. Oh, they don't do it to my face, of course. The hammering comes in the form of prayer requests and words of "concern" behind my back.

I understand the rejection, disdain, and judgment of others, and I've had to deal with my own self-condemnation because, yes, I've sinned. I've failed. I'm a hypocrite. My sins have hurt others, and that grieves me. But whether anyone likes it or not, Jesus doesn't reject, disdain, or condemn me. He's forgiven me forever, as David said, "As far as the east is from the west, so far has He removed [my] transgressions from [me]" (Psalm 103:12).

Yes, the grace of God is my shield against those who would weigh me down with their accusations. I'm grateful God has forgiven me. I pray he helps me forgive those who would deny me the love he's already shown. I know my sins and my failures are worthy of grieving.

My sins aren't worthy of guilt or shame, though, for I live in Christ.

a cup of sanity

Sometimes I think I'm crazy.

I'm so unsure what others might be saying about me. I hate the way everyone gets quiet when I come into the room. My spouse says I'm imagining things. But I worry so much about what others think about me or might do to me or how they make me feel.

In the moments when I'm indifferent to what others think, I actually feel sane again. That's when I really don't mind if others disagree with me, buy into my ideas, think I'm cool, or pity me. When I'm sane, I not only don't care what others think of me—I don't even care what I think of myself! Other-acceptance and self-acceptance aren't issues for me when God-acceptance is the big deal. That's when the Holy Spirit whispers in my ear how much God loves me despite anything that anybody, anywhere, anytime, for any reason may think about me.

> When Jesus is my center of gravity,
> I'm not only less crazy—
> I can face the world.

a cup of devotion

I'm almost afraid to believe that God loves me as much as he does.

I mean, honestly, why does he stick with me no matter what? Whether I sin, turn my back on him, hate my children, my spouse, and my neighbors, or even curse his name, he just keeps on loving me. The incredible depth of God's grace astonishes me; I can hardly believe that Jesus won't stop loving me, won't ever leave me. Am I really that precious to him? Is grace really that amazing?

I begin to get a little better idea of God's love when I think about how much I love my own children. Sure, I get angry at them, frustrated with them, and even disappointed by them, but I never stop loving them, not for a single minute. Nothing they do changes the fact they are my children, for always.

So that's how God loves me?

> Thank God he gives me this love for others, so that I'll believe how Jesus just won't stop loving me!

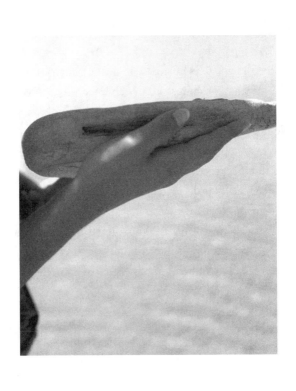

a cup of direction

Life is so confusing.

I could use a few steppingstones to guide me; otherwise the fast currents of my days threaten to sweep me to one side or the other and even carry me away.

If only I could wake in the morning and stand on truths, like stones in a river, that could lead me across the chaos in my life. How different would the day go if I could…

- keep ever mindful of my true condition before a holy God
- confess my sin and receive his grace
- accept the freedom to be human without the shame of humanity
- incline my heart to know him better
- serve others with a thankful heart

Life doesn't have to suck me into a swirl of chaos. I can be steadied atop these five bedrocks of my faith, and God has given me a Comforter to lead the way.

a cup of noise

Noise helps me keep God at bay.

I do love noise. As soon as I start the car, I reach for the radio, and the television is always on in the house. Noise keeps my head and my heart from talking with each other. After all, the things they say about me are troubling, and then I have to work harder to deny them or rationalize them.

Worse, if I stop the noise, won't God start shouting at me? Won't he just tell me to try harder, do better, do more—do, do, do?

But what if, in the quiet, God were to whisper that it's okay— that he loves me just as I am? What if he simply wanted to be quiet with me?

> God does want to have a
> quiet conversation with me,
> and it will be good.

a cup of powerlessness

Accepting my neediness feels unchristian somehow, and I rail against it.

I've said it before: I want to be strong, not weak. I like boasting about the promises I've kept. I like being the poster boy for virtuous determination. I want to feel powerful, competent, and spiritually potent so I can feel good about myself. I like daring to be a Daniel!

When I'm told that the gospel starts by my acknowledging my neediness—a condition that will continue until the day I see God— I'm a little put off. I don't like the ring of that. I'd prefer the good news to be my road map to "victory over sin" and all the troubles of my life. Good news for me is about power.

But what if the true gospel is actually about setting me free to accept my neediness? Could I finally stop competing with others? Could I finally be honest? Could I rest?

What a relief that would be.

Accepting my neediness lets me
rest in God's strength.

a cup of
companionship

*Trying so hard leaves me feeling alone
and abandoned.*

My friends say that too. Something's definitely wrong. As Christians we're called to run the good race but—good grief!—ours seem like sprints that we do all by ourselves. Our spiritual legs are burning, we're parched, and we have charley horses. Yet our churches urge us on, demanding more meetings, more witnessing, more Bible reading. More.

I feel like I'm struggling far beyond my training. Instead of accompanying the Spirit on my journey, I'm lurching ahead. If I've demanded more of myself than the Spirit enabled, I'd actually lose spiritual fruit—and that's exactly what's happening. I'm too exhausted to exhibit anything that resembles love, joy, peace, patience, and the rest. But fruit is more important than performance.

The truth is, I'm called to be *led* by the Spirit (Roman 8:14), not called to sprint ahead! He really does offer me seasons of rest, times to wait on his enabling grace. He wants me to accept the faith to do nothing and the wisdom to know when.

Thank you, Lord, for keeping by my
side, just where I need you.

a cup of holiness

I feel so much pressure to be perfect.

Perfectionism is easily confused with excellence and with an expected standard in business, academics, sports, and certainly in our Christian walk. Excellence definitely has its place. I'd prefer an excellent surgeon and an excellent pilot, and I'm glad to have an excellent wife.

But obsession with excellence can be a dangerous thing, because perfectionism is always hiding right around the corner. Perfectionism is bad, a sin of pride. Its impossible demands ruin relationships, careers, families.

If not checked by an honest appraisal of shortcomings, limitations, and sins, perfectionism will lead to blindness, denial, perpetual disappointment, anger, depression, and frustration.

That's not the life that my perfect Savior wants for me.

Jesus invites me to live by the liberating power of humility, which presupposes the inability to be perfect. Humility is evidence of the Spirit at work in me. He gives me his perfection as if it were my own—it's what makes me holy in the eyes of God.

> I really can relax, knowing that
> God sees me as perfect because
> Jesus lived the perfect life for me.

a cup of happy

If life could only be easier, I'd be happy.

Happiness = easy?

I've unwittingly and frequently believed that lie. As long as I think that *easy* will make me happy, I'm in a snare and happiness will elude me.

The whole world wants *easy*, and it's hard not to be tempted by the ads on TV. You know, the ones that say money and success, good health and independence will make life *easy* and therefore happy.

Well, suffering doesn't necessarily bring happiness, and good health can make things easier. But happiness and *easy* aren't related any more than happiness is related to money, success, or even to more noble things like sacrifice. Happy isn't the end-all of life anyway.

But it sure is nice to be happy, and there's nothing wrong with it. It's just important to remember where real happiness comes from.

Happiness = enjoying Jesus.

a cup of
contentment

Anger is hard for me to manage.

I'm angry a lot and at nearly everybody. Sometimes it makes me feel good—so right, superior, and even godly. Of course, sometimes I don't like being angry at all; I feel ashamed of losing my temper and frustrated to have my feelings revealed.

Anger is rooted in disappointment, and life has plenty of that. Disappointment is all about things not going the way I think they should, and that's all about my pride. I demand that life go my way—the right way. When it doesn't, my rage boils over or I get depressed, moody, miserable.

I wish I could say I only get angry on others' behalf or that my anger is always righteous. Frankly, I doubt it's ever righteous, because I'm not all that righteous except for when I'm being *self*-righteous!

But what if I began to believe that God really does manage the world the way it's supposed to be? Could I let my anger be pointed only at the Evil One? Would I be given the grace to allow for disappointment without closing my fist in rage?

What a relief! Believing that God's in charge helps dissolve the anger that consumes me.

a cup of life

I wonder how life's supposed to be.

Immature Christians seem to think the Christian life can be easy—that they just need to try a little harder to do a lot better. I can spot my fellow try-harder-to-do-better Christians by their nervous tics and long bootstraps. They take lots of aspirin, and they're tough to be around.

Awakening Christians aren't so sure this is the way the Christian life is designed. Awakening Christians have tried pretty hard and found that nothing's really "worked." They have baggy eyes and stare a lot.

Maturing Christians see the Christian life as a disaster unless they've gotten out of the way—they've given up trying to be better at life. They're scarred veterans of life's realities, and they know that the Christian life is completely different when the Holy Spirit is doing the living through them. I see these folks dancing from time to time; some smile a lot. Hmm. They laugh more and try less. They make way for God, Jesus, and the Spirit.

Troubles and failures, grace and joy...
that's the way life's supposed to be.

a cup of redemption

The consequences of my sin are
deeply troubling.

Like a boulder dropped into a pond, sin sends waves in all directions, and the sounds of them crashing on the shoreline seem to never stop. I've disappointed my friends, wounded those who love me, put others in awkward positions, and modeled behaviors that I pray are never imitated by my children.

I'm too often obsessively bound to the effects of my sins.

I need to consider the sovereignty of God. The same God who grants me grace in forgiveness also controls the effects of my sins. He's in the business of redeeming evil for good. He's quite remarkable at it.

Not sure about that? Consider the most extreme example: the consequence of mankind's evil is the crucified Christ. Yet that consequence redeems us and the whole creation for his glory.

> God's sovereign love overwhelms
> even our evildoing.

a cup of rest

I'm a hopeless fixer.

I live like I'm the mighty Atlas, like the world is my problem and I'm the one to carry it on my shoulders. If someone has a problem, I fix it. No wonder I'm tired. Even when shown how wrong my thinking is, I answer, "Okay, now how can I fix my thinking?"

Good grief, what a mess I am!

Isaiah 9:6 reminds me that the rule of the world, even my little world, is for Christ to bear, not me. He's the fixer, not me. Why is that so hard for me to believe? Maybe I don't want to believe. Maybe I like the way fixing things makes me feel. Maybe I believe that only I fix things the right way, which is my way.

Or maybe I believe that I'm *supposed* to fix the world. If that's true, I've been handed a terrible burden.

Lord, help me. Remind me every day that you are the sustainer of your world. Let me relax in knowing that you can fix even me! Amen.

The world rests where it belongs— on the broad shoulders of the Lord.

143

a cup of
God's presence

I feel surrounded by trouble.

And why not? There does seem to be danger everywhere: The nations are on the brink of something bad. The culture is self-destructing. My life feels dysfunctional most of the time. There are reasons to feel wary—and the Bible is clear about the forces trying to destroy any one of us at any time: The world seeks to destroy the Christian's cultural system. The flesh—the self within each of us—demands to be served. The Evil One, Satan, and the mysterious world of dark power wants dominion at our expense.

No wonder I feel enclosed by danger.

But while I may feel enclosed by danger, I'm not really trapped, because the Bible is also clear about who's standing by me, protecting me: The heavens, with legions of angels, surround me. The Holy Spirit dwells in me. The Trinitarian God—Father, Jesus, and Holy Spirit together—rule over all things and are preparing my final deliverance.

It's okay to feel threatened, but I'm not alone and not without defenders.

a cup of openness

I'm afraid to be honest with God.

Much of the time I'm resentful, disappointed, even angry with him, and then I feel guilty about it. The message I get from some Christians, however, is that I'm supposed to be always thankful and happy and how dare I be angry with God!

That's confusing to me when I look at King David of the Bible. Wasn't he often frustrated? Wasn't he angry with God sometimes too? Didn't God love him dearly anyway?

Am I not a child of God, just like David?

Imagine any parent whose child is furious with him or her. Would the parent want the child to hide anger? to pretend there's no tension, no problem? Or would a parent want such an authentic relationship in which the child is free to cry out? Isn't honest expression like David's better than pretending? Isn't a rant better than indifference, better than ignoring real feelings altogether?

The truth is, dishonesty is always disrespectful. And my heavenly Father wants me to be open and honest with him even when I'm angry.

God loves me enough to want to hear
exactly what I'm feeling.

a cup of feel-good

Feeling that I'm good enough is tough.

What is "good enough" anyway? I used to never feel good enough for my spouse, my kids, my friends, and especially God. I responded in lots of ways that usually involved doing and doing and doing. That was tiring and depressing, and the effort often left me angry.

The truth is, I'll never be good enough for God. When I read the gospels, I see how Jesus kept raising the standard for people in order to prove that very point. Remember the wealthy young ruler, the one who thought he was pretty good...until Jesus told him to go and sell everything he had and give the money to the poor? The young ruler couldn't go quite that far. None of us can, because Jesus commands all of us to be perfect, even as our Father in heaven is perfect (Matthew 5:48).

But Jesus's teaching isn't about working harder. His impossible commands are intended as something exactly to the contrary—to teach us that only he can be good enough.

Isn't that good news? All his goodness is given to me as his free gift when I trust in him. That's when I'm good enough for God.

What a relief!

Not feeling good enough is barely on my mind, because sometimes I actually feel great!

a cup of stillness

I'm so busy I could scream.

Busyness controls my life, defines who I am, determines the course of my day, and guides the decisions I make. I complain about being busy, but the truth is that I choose to be busy. Busyness gives me a sense of value. It lets me get a lot done…but it does something else too. Busyness protects me from the discomfort of stillness, that awful lull in which my soul starts to cry out for attention.

That's why I've given my life to Busy. I'd actually be ashamed to turn away from it. After all, don't responsible adults seize every moment to "do" something anyway? Don't responsible Christians exhaust themselves in ministry activities for the glory of God? Where did I get these ideas? Does activity really define me? Or does Jesus define me (2 Corinthians 5:14)?

Yes, Jesus offers me the freedom to be controlled by him instead of an agenda I set. Exhausting myself under the bondage of Busy is not the call of the gospel. Hiding in activity is not a healthy way to live.

I think I'll take a chance on stillness. I think I'll throw away the agenda for one day.

After all, I can let Busy control me or I can give in to Jesus's control.

a cup of salvation

Guilt steals my joy.

Satan likes that. He wants two things for me: blindness and paralysis. He'd prefer that I be blind to my selfish motivations, uncharitable expectations, and all the rest of my sin. Not seeing sin keeps me going along in bondage without really knowing why.

But if Satan can't keep me blind to it, when a whopper gets put on the big screen, plan B shows up. His plan B is to paralyze me with guilt. I wring my hands, hate myself, mope around feeling very sorry about the whole business—but he keeps my pride intact so that I'm stuck beating myself up instead of going all the way and accepting God's forgiveness.

I need to ask the Holy Spirit to protect me from Satan's two-pronged strategy. I need to ask him to keep my eyes open to my mountain of sin and to help me fall on my knees to be freed by his grace. Feeling guilty simply means I'm sorry enough to try harder. But I need the Spirit to teach me to truly confess, to let go of myself, and show me the immeasurable wonder of God's forgiveness.

Accepting forgiveness renews
the joy of my salvation;
it emboldens me to live again.

a cup of friendship

Worry is a companion I wish I could get rid of.

It follows me everywhere. I don't tell others, but I think they must see it on my face. I have wrinkles by my lips because they're always pursed. My forehead is starting to look like a plowed field. I'm looking like an old man. You get the picture.

I wish I could just believe that God is who he says he is. But, honestly, when I look around, it's hard for me to believe that he's in charge, and I don't really believe that he knows what's best for me. I guess that makes me a bad Christian.

I worry about that too.

Then sometimes—not often enough—I really do feel the Spirit as my companion instead of Worry; that's when I can feel secure, smile, relax. That's when I can call on the name *Immanuel*—God with us—and know I have a real friend by my side.

How good, as promised in John 14, that Immanuel sends his Spirit to be my companion, comforter, and friend—understanding my worry and helping me to cast all my burdens (including Worry) upon him so he can give me rest.

How amazing that the Comforter walks with me and can push Worry aside.

a cup of
self-awareness

My sin disgusts me and leaves me frustrated.

When I consider my sins, I'm disgusted by them; I'm sad that I wound my patient Father. But I'm also frustrated that I didn't live the Christian life well.

Who knew there is a difference here? Grieving leaves me humbled, soft, open to the power of the Spirit; being frustrated doesn't.

I have to admit that I'm mostly disgusted by failing to live the Christian life well because I hate to lose face, even with myself. Only someone who's disgusted instead of broken stays frustrated, depressed, and shamed—and I'm all these things. Only someone who's disgusted lives a life of trying harder, like me. And that's the point, because the truth is that being disgusted and frustrated, instead of grieved, tells me that my Christian life is really…about me.

At least now I can see what I'm dealing with; I can confess this for what it is. Being humbled hurts a little, but soon I'll be free to instead grieve my sin of being bound to frustration.

Thank goodness humility breaks the bondage of frustration and disgust.

a cup of confidence

Bad decisions are terrifying.

I've made more than my share, and I can tell you that I feel such terrible pressure to make good ones. Making a bad decision exposes my stupidity, my bad judgment, even my spiritual immaturity; bad decisions are the ruin of bargain addicts, success worshipers, and life managers like me.

I'm very much aware that all my life I've been under bondage to make good decisions—this bane is the root of everything from my money-management style to my vacation planning. People expect me to make good decisions every day, and frankly, that expectation makes it hard to make any decision.

The good news is that God loves me even when I make a bad decision. I'm actually free to make bad decisions! Just knowing this lets me relax—and knowing that I've never made a decision that he didn't allow is a big help too!

> I don't need to be so uptight about a potentially bad decision, nor so devastated by an actual one, because my confidence is in him.

a cup of confession

Lord, I've stolen your name to serve my Self.

I've wanted a reputation of purity, so I keep your laws impeccably. I've wanted to be remembered as a champion of the cross, so I teach your Word whenever I can. I've wanted to be known as wise, so I push my counsel on any who will listen. When others think of Jesus, I want them to think of me; when others talk of holiness, I want to be their example. I want to be known for my vast knowledge of Scripture. I've wanted power and blessings to inflate my reputation.

I've used you to get what I want for myself. I tithe, obey, pray, read my Bible, witness to others, am hospitable and charitable, and work hard at exhibiting the fruit of your Spirit.

But I haven't enjoyed you, haven't loved you. I've used you to make me look and feel better. How is it possible that you forgive me when I've stolen your name for my Self?

Your grace leaves me stunned, astonished, and in awe. I have no words but "thank you"—for loving me when I haven't loved you, for pursuing me in spite of my self-worship, for being jealous for my affections, for forgiving me when so often you've not been the object of my life but the means to other ends.

> I am the thief hanging by your cross,
> and you continue to love me.

a cup of relief

I wish I didn't get so easily discouraged.

The truth is, it's impossible to be discouraged unless I've decided what's best for me. It's impossible for me to fear the coming day unless I'm determined to manage every detail, each step along the way, on my own. It's impossible for me to worry unless I've decided what the outcome needs to be.

What a relief to know that I'm free to simply follow Jesus. "The mind of man plans his way, but the LORD directs his steps" (Proverbs 16:9).

I'm so glad Jesus invites me to follow in his steps and leads me on a journey of joy.

a cup of
desperate wonder

Is there never an end to trying harder?

When I fail at something, the first thing I usually do is resolve to try harder the next time. I'm rarely willing to admit inability; I stubbornly believe I can overcome that sin or climb that mountain.

Why is it that I'm not completely undone by the bad things I've done and the good things I've not done? Why have I believed that the answer to my failures is found in claiming "victory over sin" and that the response to sin is to grab those spiritual bootstraps and pull hard?

Yes, I'm usually sorry for my sin, but when I respond with resolutions, accountability programs, seminars, and self-help instead of collapsing at the cross, I'm on a very different path than the gospel. What a shame for me.

The gospel is intended to lead broken people to freedom.

What if I asked the Holy Spirit to take me beyond my schemes and into the wilderness of desperation, where nothing can rescue me but the free grace of God?

Jesus wants to teach me the futility of my Self—to let go of my bootstraps and hang on to the cross instead.

a cup of
responsibility

I'm tired of always being responsible.

I told that to a friend who answered, "Good. Now there's hope."

I know I should live responsibly. But my friend understood that I suffer from something else—an obsessive attachment to an exaggerated sense of responsibility that warps me into a little self-declared messiah. I exhaust myself trying to carry everyone else's (including Jesus's) burdens. I compulsively manage others' lives and feel guilty when they fail.

The causes are many. Sometimes I think too highly of myself or too little of others. Sometimes I'm addicted to control. Sometimes I'm just scared to death of failing. Other times I just think that's what's expected.

I've come to realize this isn't a responsible way to live. My inflated sense of responsibility is unhealthy, despite seeming so noble, so sacrificial, so loving on the surface. Admitting this dangerous excess to God is the truly responsible thing to do; my first step toward freedom is trusting Christ.

Responsibility begins with honesty and ends with Jesus.

a cup of want-to

*The desires of my heart seem
out of my control.*

What makes me feel good tells me a lot about myself—and sometimes even about what I worship. Do I feel good when everything is in order? Then maybe I worship order. Do I feel good when I have approval, comfort, or sensual pleasure? Then I probably worship those things.

How do I feel when I'm around Jesus?

St. Augustine reminds me in his *Confessions* that I'm not designed to change my own wants. I can't change my heart's desires—only God can. Philippians 2:13 tells me, "For it is God who is at work in you, both to will and to work for His good pleasure." This is important because I feel guilty about my desires when they are beyond my control. That's why I can't make myself feel better around Jesus any more than I can decide to prefer vanilla over chocolate.

But I can tell my Father the truth about my feelings—and I can be changed from outside myself. I can confess the other things that make me feel so good and ask the Holy Spirit to help me feel better around Jesus. That's when I'll be worshiping him again.

No, I cannot change my own desires,
but thank goodness he can change me.

a cup of warning

I feel good about my virtue, and I'm uneasy about that.

It's good that I'm uneasy with that. I need to beware of all the good qualities of life, like devotion, sacrifice, duty, and honor. I need to watch out for courage, be wary of the fruit of the Spirit. And while I'm at it, I need to be careful with that Bible I'm holding.

It is virtue, not vice, that can be the greater danger for me. It's just too easy for me to focus on all these things instead of on their Source. When I obsess over virtue, spiritual fruit can become an idol. Loving Scripture instead of the living Word can easily pervert the Bible into a thing I worship. It's just too easy for me to crave anything other than Jesus.

So I'm not going to obsess about virtues. As Jesus says in Matthew 6:33, why don't I first seek the kingdom of God (Christ) and let him add the power of virtue into my life? It's better that way.

> "My" anything should have
> a warning label.

a cup of already

I do all the right things, so where are my blessings?

Some years ago I heard a TV preacher say that if I gave more money to his ministry and lived a more obedient life, God would soon heap material blessings all over me as my reward. I just needed to write checks, behave better, and wait with an expectant heart.

So I sent in my checks; I became obsessive about godly living. I even wondered if I should borrow money to mail him in order to really prove my faith! Not much happened.

But when I thought about it more, I became angry at that preacher…and at myself. God's blessings are not for sale. We don't need to pry good things from his hand. Do we really think he's holding out on us?

So, where are my blessings?

My name is *already* written in heaven; the Holy Spirit *already* indwells me; I am *already* an heir to the kingdom of God. I am *already* his beloved child. I don't need to bribe God; Christ has opened the floodgates of God's grace.

> Jesus has already blessed me
> with all that I need.

a cup of prayer

Prayer is a struggle.

Of course it is. Prayer is about believing, and believing isn't natural. Since I struggle to really believe, I don't pray, at least not with enthusiasm, and then I feel guilty. But I need not feel guilty. True belief isn't hard—it's impossible! That's why I'm given the story of the father who pleads for his child by crying out to Jesus, "I do believe; help my unbelief" (Mark 9:24). So instead of feeling bad about not believing "enough" to pray, I can confess my unbelief and ask for the gift of faith so that I truly can believe (Ephesians 2:8).

Then, when I'm not sure what or how to pray, it helps me to remember that the disciples had the same problem. Like them, I can also ask Jesus to teach me how to pray. And just in case I think I'm not doing very well, the Bible tells me that it's really the Spirit who prays through and for me anyway: "In the same way the Spirit also helps our weakness; for we do not know how to pray as we should, but the Spirit Himself intercedes for us with groanings too deep for words" (Romans 8:26).

The faith to believe is a gift, not a skill.

Prayer may always be a struggle, but with the gift of faith, prayer can be a joy.

a cup of care

I fear pain.

I'm a world-class pain avoider. I want easy, predictable, controllable events. I'll do most anything to avoid disappointment and confusion. I struggle to fill deep needs so that I won't feel pain. But what my heart wants may or may not be what I need.

Sometimes I think I need changed circumstances to protect me from pain, yet what I really need is a changed heart. Unfortunately, heart transplants are painful.

The truth is, I have perfect circumstances today because the Architect of my circumstances is perfect and does all things well. What I have today is exactly and precisely what I need—not necessarily what I want, but certainly what I need. And that's the point: sometimes pain is what I need.

> Thank goodness God doesn't always give me the circumstances I like but takes me by the hand into precisely what I need.

a cup of health

I'm ashamed to admit my depression.

Even Christians struggle with depression, and most of us are ashamed to admit it. Sometimes we take pills or see counselors. Imagine that. Sometimes it's a simple matter of body chemistry for which we're severely and unfairly judged; other times depression is rooted in spiritual things.

Frankly, considering the pressures put on us by many Christian leaders, it's a wonder that most Christians aren't depressed.

Depression is usually caused by repressed anger and often tangled up with wrong expectations. We have good reasons to be angry, because we know our limitations. We get depressed by false teaching because we've been handed impossible missions of perfection with shaming threats attached.

On the spiritual side, much of our depression comes from imagining that Christian leaders and God are thinking the same way. Yes, of course God wants us to be a holy people, but he knows we are sinners too (1 John 1:10). He lives in our reality.

Depression can stem from anger, but I don't have to be angry with God for demanding more than I can give. He's taken care of that through Jesus.

a cup of power

Power eludes me, and I want it so desperately.

Sometimes it's good that it eludes me, because I all too easily become a power junkie. But *through Christ* I can be a powerful witness to the powerful love of a powerful God. I just need to be careful that my "power" is not *my* power...because I don't have any meaningful power beyond God in me. That's the good news of the gospel that sets me free to live very differently.

Drawing on Jesus's life and living by his Spirit, I can offer the world a powerful glimpse of his love. I do well to consider these truths that Jesus showed us:

- To feel free, live for something larger than myself
- To be bold, remember I am the much-loved son of the Creator
- To make a difference, take a risk
- To feel joy, show mercy

How exhilarating to know that real power is the Spirit living the life of Jesus through me.

a cup of certainty

Uncertainty makes me nervous.

I'm a world-class uncertainty minimizer. I want to be able to look down the road and see how everything is going to fall into place. I want to know the future so I can relax—or at least be braced for the certainty of what's coming. But I find uncertainty avoidance to be exhausting. It's just so hard to be certain in such an uncertain world.

What if I looked past the uncertainty of this life to the certainty of the next? If I spend a few moments each day considering how certain I am that my name is written in heaven—that God will redeem his creation, that there will be a new heaven and a new earth—wouldn't everything else pale in comparison? With the promises of God in view, why should I care so much about surprises here and now?

Confidence in the end of things
changes the way I deal with
the uncertainty of today.

a cup of abandon

Irritability is a problem for me.

Like all irritable people, I'm hard to love and have a hard time loving others. My attention is consumed by circumstance awareness; I'm in a constant state of agitation, frustrated by what's happening outside of my control.

I don't like being this way—it makes me feel like a spoiled child. But when life doesn't go my way, I often feel afraid, sometimes deprived, ignored, rejected, helpless. I get very irritable.

Jesus invites me to abandon that, to leave behind my Self and come to him for rest (Matthew 11:28). This means I can give him my fears and my pain, that I can surrender the management of my circumstances to him. He has come so that I might have an abundant life (John 10:10), not one of unredeemed pain and irritability.

Jesus has set me free from depending on circumstances to bring me joy.

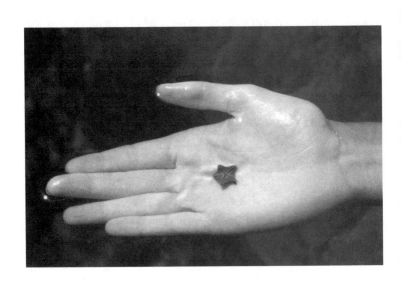

a cup of meekness

I'm so tired of trying to be mighty.

Blessed are the mighty? Isn't that the message we've all grown up with both inside and outside the church? Isn't that what we look for in a Christian leader, what we unconsciously work toward in ourselves? Doesn't the church insist that we be strong and victorious? How many Christian books urge us toward spiritual competence, Christian muscularity?

What happened to Paul's humble awareness that God's strength is made perfect in his (and our) weakness (2 Corinthians 12:9)?

Listen to Psalm 146:5–6: "Blessed is he…" who is confident, mighty, self-reliant? No. "Blessed is he whose help is the God of Jacob, whose hope is in…" his own ability, plans, resources? Not hardly. "Blessed is he whose help is the God of Jacob, whose hope is in the LORD his God, who made heaven and earth, the sea and all that is in them; who keeps faith forever."

The need to be heroic is a problem. It puts pressure on me to be what I'm not; it makes me blind to the truth about myself and others. It makes Jesus small in my life. It's a deception that leaves me surprised and confused when high-profile church leaders fail…and when I fail. Instead of being heroic, I need to be honest.

When I'm honest, I know that I'm not strong, but that's okay because Jesus is.

a cup of goodness

I wish life felt good more often.

I'm not just talking about good times. I mean *good* as in genuine, satisfying, complete, whole. Of course there are moments of good, even in the face of tough circumstances, and I live for those moments.

One morning I watched the sun come out of the Atlantic horizon. A few dolphins arced their way above flat, shimmering water. A compact wedge of sturdy pelicans paddled the air just above my head. The sky was heaven's blue. That new day felt as fresh and hopeful as I've ever known. Whole. Good. I thought of Genesis 1—"In the beginning God." These are encouraging words, especially when God goes on to declare his whole creation, like my little spot on the beach, to be "good." But just as wonderful is knowing that God continues to sustain his creation with fresh beginnings every day, even when the days don't feel so great.

How good would life be if I could see every day as that morning on the beach, if I could feel as good in his eyes as the days the earth was created? For each day and each moment in each day is a new beginning in which God is at work sustaining us, loving us, forgiving us, laughing with us, and crying with us.

How comforting to know that God declares us, and each and every day, to be good.

a cup of goal management

I'm worn out from trying to reach the goals of my life.

Whenever goal keeping characterizes my day, I find that I am intense and joyless. Goals make my life hard. They often become an end in themselves instead of useful tools. Goal keeping even becomes a way that I measure my worth; it keeps me focused on the destination instead of the journey.

I've learned the hard way that goal obsession is not freedom.

Jesus came that I might live a very different way. His purpose for my life is characterized by hopes, not goals. Hopes are not demands, not measurements, not burdens; they reveal direction for my life and show me what to long for. Yet, unlike goals, hopes demand nothing of me.

Living a life set free to hope is living a life of joy.

a cup of
vulnerability

I'm afraid to let others see my faults.

No one really wants to be exposed to others. Who likes to be embarrassed anyway? Would you want your neighbor to know that you can't manage your money? Would you tell the church that your marriage is in trouble?

Probably not. We work so hard at believing that we're not so terrible, that we're really pretty good people—not failures, at least not in Technicolor ways. The Bible reminds us that "the heart is more deceitful than all else and is desperately sick; who can understand it?" (Jeremiah 17:9). Sadly, if we're afraid to expose our hearts, others will never know us. Yet they need to witness our failures. If we don't share our faults, we deny others the security of knowing that they are not the only ones who fail.

God can open our eyes to our own failures. And he can embolden us to wisely share what we find.

Exposing the truth about myself helps
set me...and others...free.

a cup of boldness

Why am I so afraid of failure?

Failure frightens me. But failure is only a bad thing when I'm afraid of it—and I do fear it. I fear failure because I don't want to be defined as one. How wonderful it would be to not care whether I fail. Indifference to failure could embolden me to take risks, to venture far beyond my comfort zone and perceived limits.

Why should I be afraid of failure anyway? Aren't I the child of the Creator? Am I not heir to God's kingdom? Will any failure change who I am? Can any failure define me as anything other than his own?

Of course not! I can believe who I am and live boldly.

I need not fear anything, for I will always be God's much-loved child.

Failure? What's that?

a cup of motivation

*I'm frustrated about my lack of interest
in spiritual things.*

I wish I could sustain my interest, but I just don't have much motivation. I read the Bible and I shrug. The preacher pounds his fist and I yawn. Prayer? Well, I say grace at supper, but otherwise…

I feel guilty, which is the only spiritual feeling I have—unless anger counts somehow.

I wish I could feel differently. The other day I read Romans 2:4, where Paul writes, "Do you think lightly of the riches of His kindness and tolerance and patience, not knowing that the kindness of God leads you to repentance?"

Yes. In my pride I've taken God's grace lightly. I've not fully understood how undeserving I am for the utterly unconditional love he has for me. I've started asking the Spirit to show me the depth of his love, which means I also must be shown the depth of my need. The result has been a flicker of gratitude, and it's beginning to light my heart with a new love for him. While I can't muster gratitude within myself, I can confess the pride and the blindness that oppose it. I can ask the Spirit to fill my heart with an awareness of his grace so that I'm filled with thanksgiving.

When I'm grateful, I find the motivation
to truly care about God again.

a cup of relaxation

Hurried, uptight, rushed, and stressed out. That's me.

How many things can go wrong in a day anyway? Just how frustrating is it to pick the wrong checkout line or have the cashier forget to bag something? And what about those nice old folks who drive slowly—don't they know I have a lot to do?

Actually these little frustrations show me something about myself. Noticing how many times in a day I mutter under my breath is helpful. A clenched jaw and shallow breathing remind me that Jesus isn't enough for me sometimes. And that tells me I have a problem, because neither a fist in the air nor colitis is a fruit of the Spirit!

Intensity is evidence of self-absorption and control addiction—two states that, left unchecked, become unhealthy for me and everyone around me.

The good news helps me settle down a little. I can confess my condition honestly and ask the Spirit for the faith that enables me to believe that he knows all about my day's duties. And just maybe I'll see how slow drivers and bad decisions are part of his agenda for my day.

Trusting God's agenda instead of my own helps me slow down a little and gives me the freedom to relax.

a cup of
discernment

I'm so confused about what to do with sin.

Admitting that is good news for two reasons: I've already named sin for what it is, and I've taken a first step toward doing something about it. Well done. I'm still powerless to conquer sin, though. So much of what I do is sinful…and so much of what I fail to do is too. Sadly, sin is as natural to any of us as breathing.

And yet Jesus conquered sin. That means I can ask the Spirit to help me bring my sin to Jesus. That's my part of the relationship. I bring the sin, and he brings the forgiveness, grace, and power I need to sin less.

I can also ask for wisdom to discern what kind of sin I'm dealing with, since sin comes in three unpleasant flavors: ignorance, frailty, and rebellion. If I'm sinning out of ignorance, I need godly instruction. If I'm sinning out of frailty, I need the empowering balm of grace. If I'm sinning out of rebellion, I need to be reminded of God's law in all its power and fury so that I'm driven to my knees, where grace is waiting. So I can pray for discernment.

Yes, sin is a very real enemy, exclusively
dealt with by the discerning Spirit and
the finished work of the cross.

a cup of the way

Can't the Christian life be simpler?

One of the church fathers, Augustine of Hippo, summarized the Christian life in simple terms, and Martin Luther later echoed him. To paraphrase: "Love God and do as you please."

That might sound rather radical at first, but when you think about it, the idea makes perfect sense. If we truly love God, what we do will be what he wants us to do.

So how do we love God?

We can ask the Spirit to show us the need for him every day and then recognize that he loves each one of us unconditionally. And we can love him because he first loved us (1 John 4:19).

Then what about living as we please?

Jesus says that whoever loves him will be pleased to keep his commands to love God and others (John 14:23). That's not a demand but an observation.

By ourselves, we're so far gone that we can do nothing more than receive his grace. And through his grace he has set us free to love him just as we are, to love others for who they are, and yes, even to love ourselves. We are the beloved sons and daughters of the King.

What a joy it can be to get out there
and live like who we are!

a cup of
thanksgiving

Lord, let me thank you.

I thank you for:
- my fear, which sends me under your wing;
- my doubt, which obsesses me with you;
- my shame, which strips me of self;
- my frustration, which exhausts my competence;
- my perfectionism which exposes my shortcomings;
- my failures, which break my heart;
- your birth, for giving value to my world;
- your life, for showing the way of your kingdom;
- your death, for cleansing sin's decay;
- your resurrection, for breaking the wall of death;
- your righteousness, imputed to me;
- your coming again to restore your creation to wholeness;
- your love, which sets me free for all eternity.

In each of these things is hope. Amen.

acknowledgments

I offer my sincere thanks to those who patiently and otherwise pointed me to both the depravity and the dignity of my humanity. My agent, Lee Hough, cannot go unmentioned. He's been an encouraging advocate who urged me into nonfiction. Many thanks to the visionary team of professionals at Waterbrook Press and Random House. Yet none of this would have been possible were it not for those unnamed persons who bravely told me their stories; I thank each one.

index of first lines

I can't live the Christian life 5

I'm tired of being so...ordinary 7

I want more out of life 9

I'm desperate for God to help me run my life 11

Suffering in the world makes me wonder about God,
       even doubt him 13

I'm afraid of what others think of me 15

Is my suffering God's punishment for my sin? 17

Rules are such a heavy burden 19

What's with my temper?!? 21

Besetting sins make me feel like I'm not a real Christian 23

I wish I were more thankful 25

I try so hard to feel great about myself 27

Life scares me. Death terrifies me 29

Self-confidence is my drug of choice 31

I just keep believing the lie 33

I can't turn off my brain 35

Needing to be right is a terrible burden 37

Please help me find more faith 39

I'm often ashamed of who I am 41

Morality is a terrible struggle 43

Sometimes I hate myself 45

Admitting weakness is so hard for me to do 47

I'm so tired of trying to figure out God 49

Life feels so heavy 51

I worry constantly about my reputation 53

I just can't admit my weaknesses 55

It's so hard to trust in Jesus 57

I don't love others well 59

My days feel impossible 61

Living the way I do must be abnormal 63

I want so desperately to be happy 65

I don't like being such a needy person 67

I am desperate for God's favor 69

Jesus sometimes bores me 71

I have trust issues 73

Will problems never cease! 75

I want so badly to feel strong 77

Complaining drives me nuts 79

I really am self-absorbed 81

Jesus is not enough for me 83

I've given up trying to determine how I can change spiritually 85

Life's so heavy I can't breathe 87

God seems silent in my life 89

I'm addicted to my ideas of Christianity. I love my
    "victorious" living 91

Denial tries to rob me 93

I pretend to be humble 95

I wish I knew what today was about 97

Why am I so obsessed with obedience? 99

I'm addicted to feeling superior 101

Success and failure are wearisome themes in my life 103

Fear is my shadow 105

Limitations bother me 107

Criticism is hard for me to take 109

I must have order in my life 111

I worry about knowing the truth 113

All things don't seem to work together for good 115

I clutch desperately to my sense of self-worth 117

I'm not going to take it anymore 119

Sometimes I think I'm crazy 121

I'm almost afraid to believe that God loves me

    as much as he does 123

Life is so confusing 125

Noise helps me keep God at bay 127

Accepting my neediness feels unchristian somehow,

    and I rail against it 129

Trying so hard leaves me feeling alone and abandoned 131

I feel so much pressure to be perfect 133

If life could only be easier, I'd be happy 135

Anger is hard for me to manage 137

I wonder how life's supposed to be 139

The consequences of my sin are deeply troubling 141

I'm a hopeless fixer 143

I feel surrounded by trouble 145

I'm afraid to be honest with God 147

Feeling that I'm good enough is tough 149

I'm so busy I could scream 151

Guilt steals my joy 153

Worry is a companion I wish I could get rid of 155

My sin disgusts me and leaves me frustrated 157

Bad decisions are terrifying 159

Lord, I've stolen your name to serve my Self 161

I wish I didn't get so easily discouraged 163

Is there never an end to trying harder? 165

I'm tired of always being responsible 167

The desires of my heart seem out of my control 169

I feel good about my virtue, and I'm uneasy about that 171

I do all the right things, so where are my blessings? 173

Prayer is a struggle 175

I fear pain 177

I'm ashamed to admit my depression 179

Power eludes me, and I want it so desperately 181

Uncertainty makes me nervous 183

Irritability is a problem for me 185

I'm so tired of trying to be mighty 187

I wish life felt good more often 189

I'm worn out from trying to reach the goals of my life 191

I'm afraid to let others see my faults 193

Why am I so afraid of failure? 195

I'm frustrated about my lack of interest in spiritual things ... 197

Hurried, uptight, rushed, and stressed out. That's me 199

I'm so confused about what to do with sin 201

Can't the Christian life be simpler? 203

Lord, let me thank you 205

about the author

C.D. Baker founded and operated an award-winning business before redirecting his career to write. He's published five historical novels, including *The List, Swords of Heaven,* and The Journey of Souls series, one volume of which earned a Christy Award nomination (*Crusade of Tears*). He splits his time between his small farm in Bucks County, Pennsylvania, where he lives with his wife, Susan, and Scotland, where he is completing a master's degree in theological studies at the University of St. Andrews.

"I've been a believing Christian since childhood," Baker says, "but it's my personal failures that have led me to the deep well of grace from which much of my writing is drawn."

Visit him online at his Web site: www.cdbaker.com.

a note on the type

This book is set in the typeface Garamond, created by the type designer, punchcutter, and publisher Claude Garamond of Paris (1480–1561). The typefaces that Garamond produced between 1530 and 1545 are considered the typographical highlight of the sixteenth century, and today his fonts are widely copied and reproduced.

The chapter or "cup" titles in this book are set in the typeface Gothic Light, a variety face of the Gothic typographic family, and recently noted by the *New York Times* as deliberately evoking the blocky, no-nonsense, unselfconscious architectural lettering that dominated the New York City and New Jersey streetscapes from the 1930s through the 1960s in building names, neon signs, hand-lettered advertisements and lithographed posters. Created by the Greenwich Village type foundry of Hoefler and Frere-Jones, this Light face of Gothic type has no embellishments like serifs and spurs, or barbs and beaks.

An interesting coincidence—discovered after settling upon the faces used in this book for the troubled soul—is that the Gotham typeface was chosen for inscription upon the Freedom Tower cornerstone at the World Trade Center site.